AF886314

Reading STREET

Grade 4

Pearson Scott Foresman Reading Street

Practice Stations Management Handbook

PEARSON

Glenview, Illinois
Boston, Massachusetts
Chandler, Arizona
Upper Saddle River, New Jersey

ISBN-13: 978-0-328-38468-6
ISBN-10: 0-328-38468-2

2 3 4 5 6 7 8 9 10 12 11 10 09
CC1

Reading STREET

Grade 4

Table of Contents

Welcome to Practice Station Time!

The Pearson Scott Foresman Reading Street Practice Stations Kit helps simplify the task of managing stations by providing ideas for setting up classroom stations, weekly activities for each station, and suggested student routines for each station.

Pearson Scott Foresman Reading Street Practice Stations Kit Components

Practice Stations Management Poster

One of the keys to making Practice Station time productive is for students to know at which station they should be working each day. With this write-on/wipe-off chart, you can label the stations for the week by attaching Practice Station icons and list students' names for each station.

Practice Station Icons

Use Practice Station Icons to tell students which stations they can visit on any particular day or week. You can apply these icons to the Practice Stations Management Poster interchangeably.

Practice Station Flip Charts

The Practice Station Flip Charts are tabletop-sized flip charts that complement the Practice Station activities in the Teacher's Edition. Each flip-chart page lists materials needed for and describes, in student-friendly language, the weekly activity for that station. There are four flip charts, one each for the following stations: Vocabulary, Writing, Science/History-Social Science, and Technology. The activities provide opportunities for students to practice skills and to expand knowledge of the weekly concept across a variety of content areas.

Setting Up the Practice Stations

The classroom environment is an important factor in students' learning. Create separate spaces for the different types of instruction and activities that take place each day.

A Stations-Friendly Classroom

As much as possible, a classroom environment should be warm, inviting, and conducive to effective learning for you and your students. As an integral part of that environment, Practice Stations should be comfortable areas in which students can work independently, in pairs, or in small groups. With this in mind, consider some or all of the following suggestions when developing your stations.

- Set aside an area for whole-class instruction and a space for you to work with small groups.
- Think about the function of each station and where it is most appropriately located in the room.
- Provide as much space as possible between noisy and quiet areas.
- Develop traffic patterns that allow for easy movement through and around stations.

One possible classroom set-up is shown to the right.

Establish Stations Routines

Practice Station time will be most effective if you develop routines and set clear expectations for students working in the stations. Following are suggestions to help students reach independence.

- Use the Management Lessons to introduce each station and model how to use them. Coach students on how to be responsible when working in the stations.
- Establish rules for each station, discuss these with students, and post them in the stations.
- Make sure that students understand what is expected of them for each station activity. Post suggestions for early finishers in each station.
- Support students in making their own decisions about what to do at a station and how to solve problems.
- Use the Practice Stations Management Poster provided so that students will know where they should be on a daily basis.
- Appoint a "stations monitor" each week whose job it is to update the management poster and make sure that students know where they should be working.
- Distribute copies of "My Work Plan" each week to help students plan their time and tasks.
- Stock each station with appropriate supplies.

Once students are using the stations, you can rotate among them, answering questions, providing direction and feedback, guiding research, and assessing student performance.

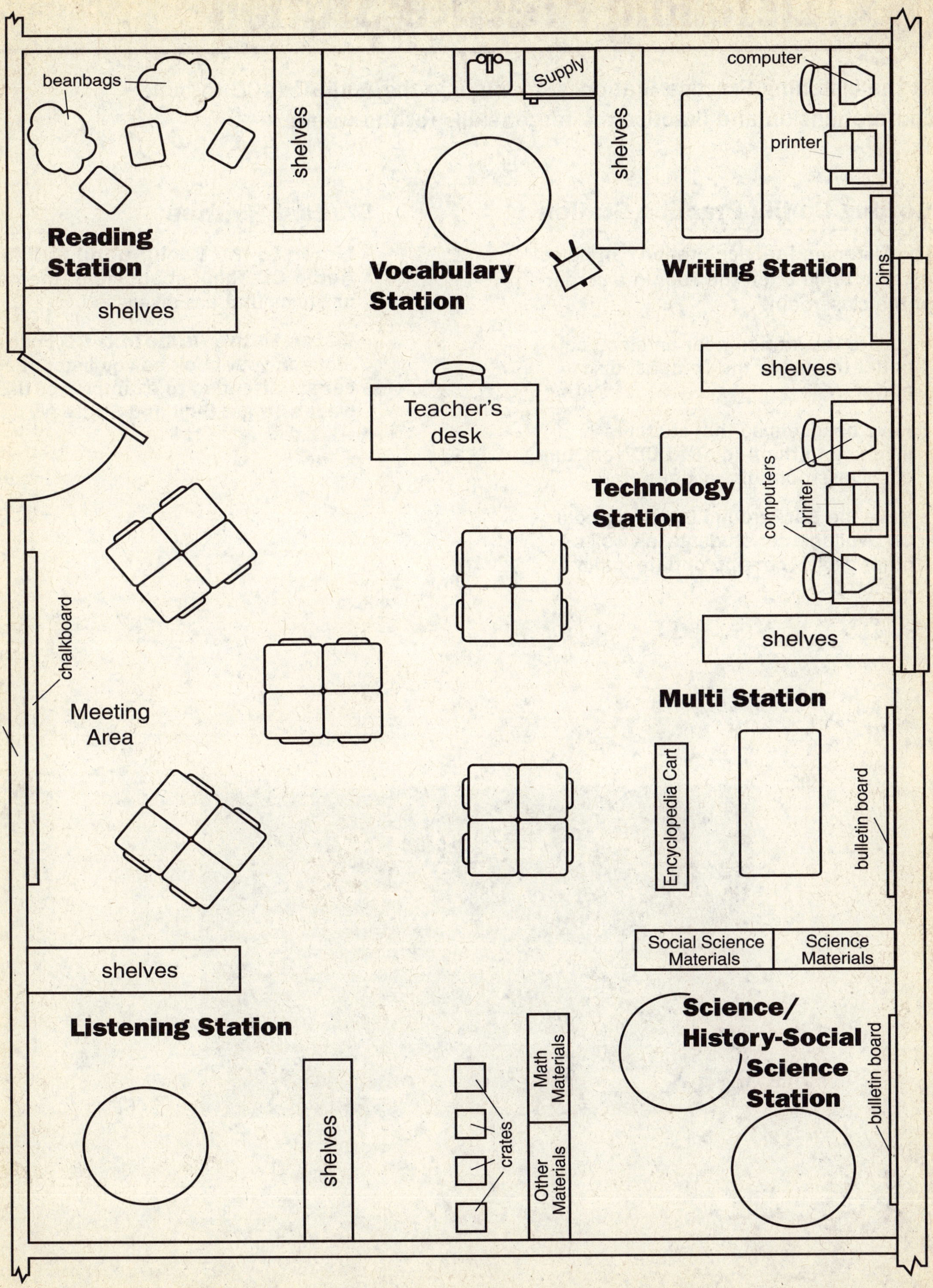
beanbags
shelves
Supply
shelves
computer
printer
Reading Station
shelves
Vocabulary Station
Writing Station
bins
shelves
Teacher's desk
Technology Station
computers
printer
shelves
chalkboard
lockers
Meeting Area
Multi Station
Encyclopedia Cart
bulletin board
Social Science Materials
Science Materials
shelves
Listening Station
Science/ History-Social Science Station
Math Materials
crates
shelves
Other Materials
bulletin board

Listening Practice Station

At the Listening Practice Station, students use the AudioText CD to build comprehension and practice the target skills for the week.

Setting Up the Practice Station

The Listening Practice Station can be set up on a table or on the floor in a corner of the classroom.

- Locate the station near an electrical outlet to plug in the compact disc player.
- Have headsets so that students listening to the AudioText CD can "tune out" classroom distractions.
- Have the Background Building Audio CD available for students, as well as other classroom-appropriate audio materials.

Student Routine

- **Listen to the Background Building Audio CD** Think about ideas, themes, or topics that are discussed.
- **Listen to the AudioText CD** Follow along in your book as you listen. Pay careful attention to examples of this week's Target Skill and Strategy.

TEACHER TiP

- Use a predictable, consistent routine when transitioning to Practice Station time. Students can then focus on the specific directions for that day instead of wondering how they are going to get there.

Listening Practice Station

Management Lesson Using Equipment

Materials class CD players, headphones, AudioText CDs

Introduce Ask students if they have CD players at home, what the devices look like, and how they work. I see most of you already know how to work a CD player. But every player is different. Today we are going to practice with the class CD players that we use for our Listening Practice Station. That way you'll be able to play the CDs there without any help.

Model Model using the listening equipment by demonstrating each step as you talk about it. Here is where I turn the player on. I press this button and watch for the red light to go on. I put my headphones directly over my ears and make sure they are plugged in right here. To open the player, I press here. See the round space inside? I take the CD out of the case carefully and fit it exactly into the round space in the player. Close the player [or push in the CD drawer], like this. I should hear the sound begin in a second or two. I adjust the volume and my headphones so that I can hear without disturbing others.

Guide practice Now it's your turn. When I call your names, come over to the Listening Station and start the CD player as I direct you. Call on as many students as you have players. Repeat the steps aloud, but let the students perform them. Allow them to listen for a moment, then ask: What do you hear? If a student misses a step, model again. Repeat until all students have had a turn.

On their own Let's all practice using the equipment. Come to the Listening Station again, but this time work the CD player for yourself. Call students as you did earlier. Circulate among them as they listen, providing feedback as necessary.

MANAGEMENT TIP

As students practice using the equipment, have them listen to this week's AudioText and follow along in their Student Books.

Reading Practice Station

At the Reading Practice Station, students can read additional material to make connections across texts; explore personal interests; or find out more about topics, authors, and genres that are related to the week's concept or theme.

Setting Up the Practice Station

Find a comfortable space for this station away from the main activity of the classroom.

- Include a table and chairs as well as rocking chairs, carpet squares, or beanbags.
- Use shelves, wire rack bins, or plastic tote trays to create an organized classroom library.
- Group books by theme, topic, genre, reading level, or author.

Student Routine

1. **Preview the Book** Read the title and look at the cover and illustrations. Think about what this book might be about. Write a prediction. Set a purpose for reading.
2. **Read the Book** If the book is **fiction**, answer questions such as these:
   - Who are the characters? What are they like?
   - When and where does the story take place?
   - What problem do the characters have? How is the problem solved? How else might it have been solved?

   If the book is **nonfiction**, think about the information you are reading. Write some facts and ideas you learn from your reading. Also write additional questions you have about the topic.
3. **Respond to the Book** If the book is **fiction**, retell the story in your own words.

   If the book is **nonfiction**, tell three things you learned about the topic.

Reading Practice Station

Management Lesson 1 Independent Reading

Materials chart paper, markers, self-selected books

Introduce Have students tell what it means to do something independently. (Possible responses: to do something on your own, to do something by yourself) Today we are going to practice how to read independently. Reading independently means reading on our own. Why is it important for us to spend time reading on our own? That's right, reading independently is enjoyable because we get to choose our own books and learn about things we find interesting. Independent reading also helps us become better readers. It allows us to practice the skills and strategies we learn in class.

Model Using a self-selected book, model reading independently. When I read independently, I sit at my desk or in the classroom library. I respect my classmates by reading silently. This way I am not disturbing them as they read independently or do other class work. I focus on my book, not on other activities that may be going on in the classroom. I quickly find my place in my book, and I read until time is up. Watch as I read. Model reading independently.

Write *Rules for Independent Reading* at the top of a piece of chart paper. What did you notice about my independent reading? As students respond, restate their observations as rules and record the rules on the chart.

Rules for Independent Reading

- Sit at your desk or find a spot where you will not be disturbed.
- Read silently.
- Read the entire time.
- Do not disturb others.
- Focus on reading your book.

Guide practice Now it's your turn. Have the group model appropriate reading behaviors. What did you notice about our reading? This is the way I want you to read independently.

On their own Let's all practice independent reading. When I call your name, take your book and find a spot where you can read without being disturbed. Make sure you are using the reading behaviors we listed on our chart. We will read for five minutes. I will let you know when time is up. Gradually dismiss individuals. As students read, circulate around the room providing feedback. If students are disturbing others, turn their attention back to their book and model focused reading.

MANAGEMENT TIP

Start off slowly, gradually increasing the amount of time students spend reading independently. Model and provide corrective feedback as necessary.

Reading Practice Station

Management Lesson 2 Choosing Appropriate Books

Materials books from the classroom library

Introduce Ask students to share the titles and genres of books they have read. Today we are going to practice choosing appropriate books. What is an appropriate book? Yes, an appropriate book is one you find interesting, or one that will be perfect for an assignment. An appropriate book isn't too hard and isn't too easy. It has just the right number of pages for you. Thinking about your reason for reading will help you choose the right book.

Model Model choosing an appropriate book. First, I think about subjects that interest me. I'm really interested in dinosaurs, so I'll look for a nonfiction book about dinosaurs or fossils. I pick out a book with a title that looks like it might be about prehistoric times. Then I look at a few pages to see if it is too hard or too easy. Read a short sample paragraph aloud. That sounds like something I can read. I like the illustrations too. I think I'll enjoy this book.

Guide practice Now it's your turn. Look at these books. Display several grade-level books and have the group offer suggestions as they consider the books. Which one would you choose if you felt like reading a funny book? Which book would choose if you wanted to learn about weather around the world? What if you had to write a biography about an American inventor? Have students look through books to determine which would be appropriate for them.

On their own Let's practice choosing appropriate books. When I call your name, go to the classroom library and pick out a fiction book to read for fun and an expository book to read for information. Take the books back to your desk and begin reading. Dismiss students three or four at a time. As students choose books, circulate around the room, looking at student choices and providing feedback. Follow your procedures for borrowing books from the classroom library.

MANAGEMENT TIP

Listen carefully to the types of books that students like so that you can make individual suggestions.

Reading Practice Station

Management Lesson 3 Using a Reading Log

Materials chart paper; markers; copies of My Reading Log, p. 64; pencils

Introduce Today we are going to practice using a reading log. A reading log is a record of books we've read. It's like a miniature book report. Why is it important to keep a record of what we've read? Yes, when we keep a reading log we always know which books we've read. A reading log can show us what books we find interesting. It can also show us how our reading has improved throughout the year.

Model Watch as I write information in this log. **Model filling in a reading log by making a quick replica of My Reading Log, p. 64, on chart paper.** I always fill out my log right when I finish reading the book. If I'm reading a long book, I fill out my log as I finish each chapter or chunk of reading.

I write my name on my reading log. Then I write today's date. Next, I think about what I read today. **Continue filling in the log, using books students might be familiar with. As you mention them, write the titles and authors on the chart paper. Point out that you are including things you've read outside of class.** The last column is where I write my opinion of, or what I thought about, the book.

Guide practice Now it's your turn. Let's make a log for the whole class. **Flip to the next blank page on the chart, and write *Our Reading Log*. After you write the date, initiate participation by writing in the Title column a selection students recently read in their Student Books. Then lead the group in completing the log. If students forget or do not know the author of the selection, have them turn to the appropriate page to find this information. For the last column, record the general opinion of the group.**

On their own Let's all practice using a reading log. Look through your Student Book or go to the class library and find a book you have already read. **Distribute copies of My Reading Log and have students create their own reading logs. As students write, circulate around the room, providing feedback.**

MANAGEMENT TIP

If students would like to add more information to their reading logs, suggest they write about their favorite part of the book, or list and describe the characters and setting. Model and give corrective feedback as necessary.

Vocabulary Practice Station

At the Vocabulary Practice Station, students will practice using the lesson vocabulary and vocabulary skills and strategies in various activities to extend and enrich their understanding of key concepts and themes. Students will also build their speaking and reading vocabularies.

Setting Up the Practice Station

- Supplement the center with other vocabulary-building activities that are language-rich.
- Use weekly spelling words with these activities to practice strategies and reinforce understanding of word meanings.

Student Routine

- **Discuss New Words** Use the vocabulary in a conversation with a partner.
- **Ask and Answer Questions** Develop questions based on the words.
- **Create Images** Think of an image that reinforces the word meaning.
- **Use New Words** Create opportunities to use new vocabulary every day.

TEACHER TiP

- Make a list of options for early finishers and post them on the board or on an overhead transparency.
- Make a "lost" jar/box so that students will know where to put stray items. These items can then be easily returned to the correct station.

Vocabulary Practice Station

Management Lesson 1 Managing Time

Materials this week's Words to Know, divided into three groups; thesauruses; clock; chart paper; pencils; paper

Introduce Today we are going to practice managing time. When we work in the Practice Stations, we have fifteen minutes to complete all the steps. If we spend too much time on one step, we won't finish in fifteen minutes. If we rush through our work, however, we are more apt to make mistakes. To be sure we get all the work done correctly, we need to manage our time.

Model **Have this assignment written on the board: 1. Write the Words to Know. 2. Look up the words in a thesaurus to find their antonyms. 3. Write the antonyms for the words next to each one.** When I begin the assignment, the first thing I do is to look at the clock. It's 1:15. That means I have until 1:30 to finish. Now I read the directions. I make sure I have all my materials—my Student Book, a pencil, paper, and a thesaurus. I begin right away. **(Do step one.)** When I'm finished with step one, I look at the clock. I have 13 minutes left. **Begin looking up each word and writing its antonym. Pause after half the words are done.** Now I look at the clock again. I'm right on time.

Write *Rules for Managing Time* at the top of a piece of chart paper. What rules did we talk about for managing time? **As students respond, record their observations on the chart.**

Rules for Managing Time

- Check the clock.
- Read the directions.
- Make sure you have all your materials.
- Begin right away.
- Go right from one step to the next without stopping.

Guide practice Now it's your turn. First look at the clock. What time is it? By what time will we have to finish? Now read the directions silently. Do we have our materials? **Lead the group in writing the second group of Words to Know, looking them up in a thesaurus, and writing their antonyms.** Look at the clock. What did you notice about how we managed our time?

On their own Let's all practice managing our time. **Have students complete the same assignment, this time using the third group of Words to Know. Have them refer to the chart you created. As students work, circulate around the room, providing feedback.**

MANAGEMENT TIP

If students are stuck on a word, have them continue to the next one and go back to the problematic one later. Model and give corrective feedback as necessary.

Vocabulary Practice Station

Management Lesson 2 Using Reference Sources

Materials dictionaries, thesauruses, pencils, paper

Introduce Today we're going to practice using reference sources. A reference source is a book or Web site we consult if we want information about something. What are some reference sources you know? **(Possible responses: dictionaries, thesauruses, magazines, online encyclopedias)** If you want to use a word correctly, you have to know all about it—what kind of word it is, what it means, how it is used, its synonyms and antonyms, and so on.

Model **Model using reference sources. Write these words on the board: *chum, exterior, sparse.*** How do I find out what these words mean? I use a dictionary. Dictionaries are reference books I use to find the definition, or meaning, of a word. **Demonstrate looking up *chum* and read its definition aloud. Explain what other information can be found in a dictionary, such as pronunciation, part of speech, and origin.** What reference source do I use if want to know another word that means the same as, or the opposite of, *chum?* Yes, I'd use a thesaurus. **Use a thesaurus to look up the word again, reading its synonyms and antonyms aloud.** I now know enough about the word to use it in an original sentence, one that I make up myself. **Now write on the board: *My <u>chums</u> and I went to the movies.***

Guide practice Now it's your turn. **Lead students in looking up the definition of *exterior* in a dictionary, and then using a thesaurus to find its synonyms and antonyms. Have the group come up with a sentence or two using the word and write it on the board.**

On their own Let's all practice using reference sources. **Have individuals look up and write the definition of, a synonym for, and an antonym for *sparse.* Then have them write an original sentence using the word. As students use reference sources, circulate around the room, providing feedback.**

MANAGEMENT TIP

Students who finish early can investigate the word even further by looking up and writing its pronunciation, its part of speech, and its origin. Model and provide corrective feedback as necessary.

Vocabulary Practice Station

Management Lesson 3 Using Graphic Organizers

Materials handouts of these graphic organizers: Venn diagram, 3-column chart, word web; Student Books; paper and pencils

Introduce Today we're going to practice using graphic organizers. What are some reasons we might use graphic organizers in the Vocabulary Practice Station? (Possible responses: to learn more about words and word structure, to help learn word definitions, to classify and categorize) Graphic organizers help keep our vocabulary work organized too.

Model Model using a graphic organizer. Write these words on the board: *beautiful, mountainous, preheat, unmanageable.* Let's say I'm studying prefixes and suffixes, and I'd like to organize a list of words by classifying them. I can use a Venn diagram. Draw a Venn diagram on the board. I'll put words with prefixes in one circle, words with suffixes in another circle, and words with both prefixes and suffixes in the middle. This graphic organizer shows what I know about prefixes and suffixes. Using the same information, continue modeling with other graphic organizers, such as a 3-column chart and a word web.

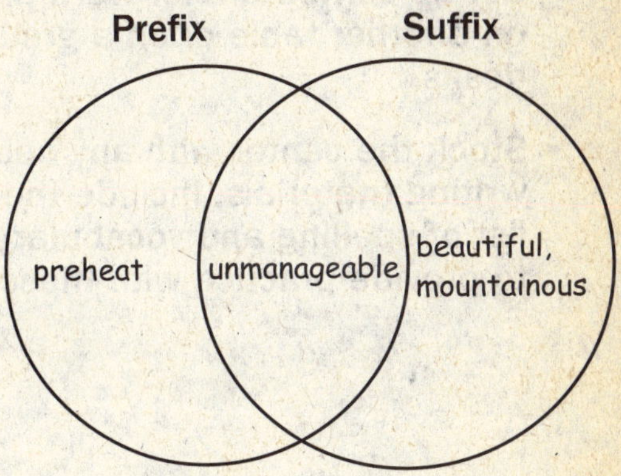

Guide practice Now it's your turn. Draw another graphic organizer. Write these words on the board: *disappearance, equipment, regain, unbelievable.* Work with the group to fill in the graphic organizer the same way you did earlier. What does this graphic organizer show? How will it help you learn more about words?

On their own Let's all practice using a graphic organizer. Have students look through their Student Books for several examples of words with prefixes, suffixes, or both. Then have them use a graphic organizer of their choice to classify the words they've found. Be sure students are familiar with how the graphic organizer works and if it is an adequate method of classifying. As students work, circulate around the room, providing feedback.

MANAGEMENT TIP

Before individuals begin their word search, write lists of familiar prefixes and suffixes on the board.

Writing Practice Station

At the Writing Practice Station, students may work on process writing activities from the Teacher's Edition or self-selected activities that relate to texts they've read. Students practice the weekly conventions skill, the writing trait, or writing subtrait.

Setting Up the Practice Station

The Writing Practice Station may need more space than others.

- Designate a table for students who are working on prewriting and drafting activities, and another for revising, editing, and publishing.
- Set up computers for word processing on another table or on a group of desks.
- Stock the center with any necessary writing materials. Include the weekly list of spelling and vocabulary words to provide practice with these words.

Student Routine

Response Journal

- **Before Reading** Make predictions about what you think will happen, or set a purpose for reading—what you want to learn or find out.
- **During Reading** As you read, stop as necessary to write difficult words and phrases, or ask questions about the topic, events, characters, or setting. Continue to check and revise your predictions.
- **After Reading** Use your journal to check your predictions. You might also write about which part you liked best and why, or compare the selection to a similar story or article you have read.

Writing Practice Station

Management Lesson 1 Working with a Partner

Materials chart paper, markers, paper, pencils

Introduce Ask students about assignments they have worked on with a partner. Was the assignment successful? Why or why not? Today we are going to practice working with a partner. Sometimes working with a partner is easy to do and sometimes it is not. When we work on our own, we make all the decisions about the work we do. When we work with someone else, we have to consider another person's thoughts and ideas. We have to cooperate and compromise.

Model Choose one student to act as your partner as you model working with a partner. Let's say I'm supposed to write a list of interrogative sentences with a partner, paying careful attention to writing conventions. How would I start? It's best to first talk about what we need to accomplish—writing the list of sentences. Then we should decide what jobs there are and who will do which job. My partner and I decide that we'll take turns thinking of sentences, but I'll be the one who writes them. Then we'll both check the list for correct punctuation and capitalization. Model writing a few sentences with your partner. As we work, we always communicate, cooperate, and compromise. Then we'll complete the activity successfully.

Steps for Working with a Partner

- Discuss the activity.
- Decide what the jobs are and divide them up.
- Cooperate, communicate, and compromise.
- Complete the activity.

Write *Steps for Working with a Partner* at the top of a piece of chart paper. What steps did we talk about for working with a partner? As students respond, record their observations on the chart.

Guide practice Now it's your turn. Pair students and lead them in working together on writing an interrogative sentence. Have the group restate the steps you've just discussed. This is how I'd like you to work with a partner.

On their own Let's all practice working with a partner. Pair students again, this time with different partners, and have them work together in writing two lists—one list of interrogative sentences and one list of declarative sentences. As students work, circulate around the room, providing feedback.

MANAGEMENT TIP

Tell students that it's okay for partners to disagree, but that they must work together politely and quietly to come up with a solution to the problem. Model and give corrective feedback as necessary.

Writing Practice Station

Management Lesson 2 Using Editing Marks

Materials three short stories or essays (two on the board, one handout) with errors prepared in advance, chart paper, markers, red pens or pencils

Introduce Today we are going to practice using editing marks. We always want to do our best work when we write reports and essays, so we write more than one draft. To do that, we go over what we have written and mark what we want to change before we rewrite it. Trying to write our own notes can get messy and crowded. Using editing marks is a shorter way to mark the changes we want to make in our writing.

Model Make a list of editing marks on chart paper and discuss each one. Then use one of the essays to model using editing marks. Read each sentence aloud before you change it. I'm going to go through the essay slowly, sentence by sentence. In this first sentence I accidentally wrote the word *the* twice. I want to get rid of, or delete, one *the.* I cross it out with a special line. In this sentence I left out the word *life* between *real* and *today,* so I make a mark between the words. It's called a caret, and even though it's not spelled like the vegetable, it looks a little like it! It's pointed like this. Above the sentence over the caret I write the word *life.* The first word in this sentence should be capitalized, so I put three lines under it. This word is misspelled, so I write *sp* in a circle. This sentence is missing a period, so I add one and circle it. Now I'm ready to rewrite my draft, incorporating the edits I made.

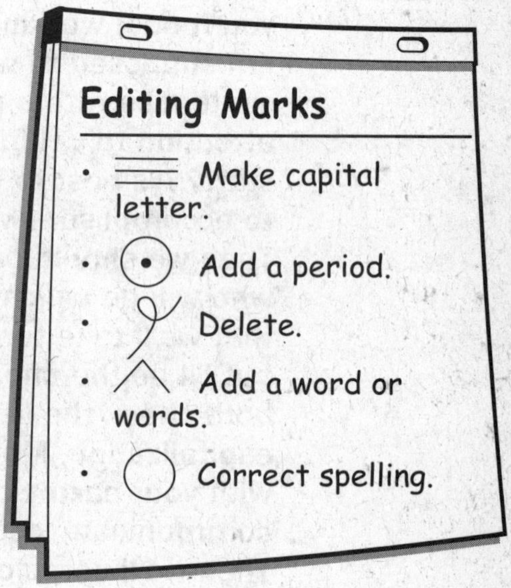

Guide practice Now it's your turn. Here's another essay. Tell me what needs correction and how I should edit. Read the sentences one at a time and write the marks at students' direction. Review the words *delete* and *caret.* Refer to the chart as necessary.

On their own Let's all practice using editing marks. Distribute copies of the third essay. Here is another piece of writing. Correct the mistakes, using editing marks. As students make corrections, circulate around the room, providing feedback. If they have time, have them rewrite the essay, incorporating their edits.

MANAGEMENT TIP

Have students use a red pen or pencil when they make editing marks. This will help them spot their edits quickly.

Science/Social Science Practice Station

At the Science/History-Social Science Practice Station, students can work individually, with partners, or in small groups to explore content area activities related to the theme or subject matter of the selections.

Setting Up the Practice Station

Provide a table where students can create content-related projects, examine maps and globes, and so on.

- Use bookshelves or bins to store reading and reference materials.
- Stock the center with a variety of materials that correspond to the content-area assignments.
- Include various reference materials for social science or science activities.
- Have manipulatives, graph paper, rulers, and any other necessary materials on hand.

Student Routine

Science

- Read the directions carefully.
- Visualize the steps first before you actually do the activity.
- Complete the activity.

Social Science

- Read any reference materials first.
- Take notes as you read.
- Use the information in your notes to complete the activity.

Science/Social Science Practice Station

Management Lesson 1 Skimming for Information

Materials grade-level science or social science trade books, Internet-connected computer with projection

Introduce Today we're going to practice skimming for information. What does it mean to skim a book? Yes, it means to look through it quickly and read only the important points. When we're conducting research, we may have several books and Web sites we can check, but we don't have time to read every single word. Skimming the material helps us find out what we want to know quickly.

Model Use a trade book to model skimming for information. Let's say I'm going to write a report about the life and times of U.S. President Franklin Roosevelt. When I skim for information about Roosevelt, I run my finger down the columns of text, and stop when I notice names, words, and key terms that seem to jump out at me, or that convey important facts about Roosevelt and his presidency. I might read the first and last paragraph on a page, or the first sentence in all paragraphs. I know that subheads, bulleted lists, and illustration captions often contain important information, so I read more thoroughly when I come across those text features. Continue modeling, reading aloud when you reach important points. In just a few minutes I've learned a lot about Franklin Roosevelt. Now I can begin my research.

Guide practice Now it's your turn. Lead the group in deciding on a topic they wish to learn more about, and then skimming for information about that topic, this time using the Internet as a reference source. When we skim for information on a Web site, we use the cursor, not our finger, to keep our place. Tell students that skimming for information takes a lot of practice—they will have to "train" their eyes to do it.

On their own Let's all practice skimming for information. Pair students and have each pair choose a science or social science trade book that interests them. Have them take turns skimming for information about a specific topic in the book, reading aloud the important points they find. As partners work, circulate around the room, providing feedback.

MANAGEMENT TIP

If students have trouble differentiating between important information and inessential information, have them write the information as they skim. Seeing isolated facts on paper can help students determine relevance. Model and give corrective feedback as necessary.

Science/Social Science Practice Station

Management Lesson 2 Recording Information

Materials copies of graphic organizers: T-chart, Venn diagram, word web; grade-level science and social science books

Introduce Today we're going to practice recording information. What are some reasons we might need information? Yes, we might need it for a report, a presentation, or a project. But just locating information isn't always enough. To use the information we need to record it in a specific way. A good way to do that is with graphic organizers. Then later we can use the information in the graphic organizers to help us write a report or do a project.

Model **Model recording information. Draw a T-chart on chart paper.** This graphic organizer is called a T-chart. I just read a book about insects and want to record the information I learned. In the book, I learned about butterflies and moths. I learned they both belong to an order of insects called Lepidoptera, so that will be the title of my chart. **Label the first column *Butterflies* and the second column *Moths*. As you talk about what you read, fill in the appropriate columns.** This graphic organizer shows the information I learned about butterflies and moths. **Continue modeling, using a Venn diagram and a word web.**

Lepidoptera

Butterflies	Moths
larvae are caterpillars	larvae are caterpillars
thin antennae	feathery antennae
rest with folded wings	rest with wings spread out
sip nectar	sip nectar

Guide practice Now it's your turn. **Draw or use another graphic organizer. Look through a science or social science book with students, finding information. Work with the group to fill in the graphic organizer with the information you found.** What does this graphic organizer show? How will it help when you write a report?

On their own Let's all practice recording information. **Have students look through books and have them record information, using a graphic organizer of their choice. Be sure students are familiar with how the graphic organizer works and if it is an adequate method of recording information. As students work, circulate around the room providing feedback.**

MANAGEMENT TIP

Tell students they do not need to write complete sentences in their graphic organizers. Model writing key points and give corrective feedback as necessary.

Science/Social Science Practice Station

Management Lesson 3 Communicating Information

Materials computer with projection and students' computers

Introduce Today we're going to practice communicating information. What does it mean to communicate? Yes, when we communicate, we share news or information about something. How do we communicate? **(Possible responses: by speaking, by writing, by drawing, by using body language)** In school, we often communicate information we've researched and recorded. We can do that by giving an oral presentation, writing a report, drawing pictures, or doing a combination of any of these.

Model **Model communicating information. Use a topic connected to the weekly concept.** First I need some information to talk about. I'll look up "Chinese New Year celebration" on the Internet. I see that the Chinese decorate their homes with the lucky color red, eat long noodles to symbolize long life, and create special banners with poems written on them. Then they light fireworks. I'll make a list of these facts. **Write on the board or open a word document.** This list communicates the information quickly. But maybe I would rather present it to the class orally. I'll need to write it, and then say it, in an interesting way. **Model communicating the same information orally, and then use computer graphics or drawings to represent each fact. Add captions.**

Guide practice Now it's your turn. Let's look up another New Year celebration, this time from Greece. **Allow students to choose which facts to use and how to list them, as you write.** Now we have our facts. How can we present them orally? **Encourage students to express the information in an interesting and correct way, as you write the sentences they create on the board. Have the group read them aloud.** Now let's choose some pictures that will show the information.

On their own Let's all practice communicating information. Research Sweden's New Year celebration and make a list of facts. Write the information as an oral presentation, and then put it into pictures with captions. You may get the pictures from the computer or draw them yourself. **As children work, circulate around the room providing feedback.**

MANAGEMENT TIP

If students do not understand how to distinguish important facts from less important ones, point out specific examples of important facts and explain how they differ from those that aren't. Monitor and give corrective feedback as necessary.

Technology Practice Station

At the Technology Practice Station, students use the Internet and other technology-based resources for research and problem solving. They use word-processing programs to create documents.

Setting Up the Practice Station

Select a place for this station where you can set up as many computers as possible.

- Post simple directions for using equipment.
- Provide quick-help cards for students to use if they get stuck.
- Include classroom or school rules for appropriate Internet use.
- Stock the center with materials appropriate to the activity for the week.
- Make sure the computer has the appropriate software for the activity.

Student Routine

Internet Inquiry

1. **Identify Questions** Identify a question or a topic you want to explore. Browse a few Web sites or print reference materials to develop an inquiry question.
2. **Navigate/Search** Conduct effective information searches and look for text and images that can help you answer your questions. Use a student-friendly search engine to conduct your own searches. Be sure to follow classroom guidelines for Internet use.
3. **Analyze** Explore Web sites or print materials. Analyze the information you have found to determine whether or not it is useful. Print or take notes on valid information.
4. **Synthesize** Combine relevant information you've collected from different sources to develop an answer to your inquiry question.
5. **Communicate** Prepare a list of useful resources for other students who may wish to explore your topic. You might also prepare a presentation about your findings.

Technology Practice Station

Management Lesson 1 Using Equipment

Materials computer with projection

Introduce Today we're going to talk about using computers. You probably already know a lot about computers. Place the computer and arrange the class in such a way that all students can see the computer or projection screen. Point to different parts and ask students what they are. Be sure to include computer, monitor or screen, mouse, keyboard, and CD holder. Point out the printer as well. We'll be using the computer to do some class assignments, so it's important to use it correctly.

Model Model using equipment. I never touch the computer with dirty or sticky hands. I use the equipment carefully, correctly, and only with permission. The first step in using a computer is to make sure it is turned on. Here's the on-off switch. When the computer is on, this switch is usually lit up. Push the switch on and off to demonstrate, then explain usernames and passwords, if applicable. Once the monitor is warmed up, I can see these little pictures called desktop icons. With the mouse I move the cursor, which is the arrow you see here, over an icon and click. Explain the icons available to students. Then exit and demonstrate how to turn the machine off.

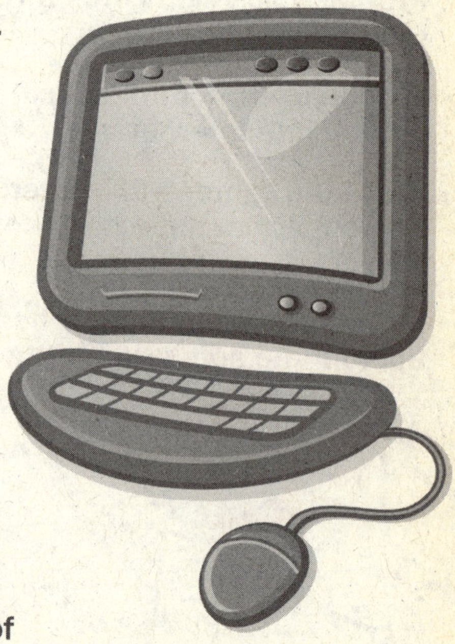

Guide practice Now it's your turn. Lead students in demonstrating how the computer is used. Go through the process of turning the computer on (and off), having the group tell you which step comes first, next, and last as you complete each one.

On their own Let's all practice logging on to the computer and using the equipment. Have the students log on and off at individual computers, taking turns if necessary. They should practice clicking on various icons until they are familiar with what is available to them. Then have students exit so the computer is ready for their classmates to use. Circulate among them, offering corrective feedback. Use the new terms they've learned as you do so.

MANAGEMENT TIP

Demonstrate slowly. Make sure students can see the mouse, the cursor, and the keyboard and how you are using them. Model and provide corrective feedback as necessary.

Technology Practice Station

Management Lesson 2 Using a Search Engine

Materials computer with projection, student computers

Introduce Place the computer and arrange the class so all students can see the computer or projection. Today we are going to practice using a search engine. What is a search engine? Yes, it's a system on our computer that helps us find information on the Internet. A search engine is an important tool we use in order to do thorough research.

Model Model using a search engine. First I make sure the computer is turned on. If it is, but the screen is blank, I tap a key on the keyboard or wiggle the mouse around. Now I can see the desktop icons. This one will give me the search engine. When I click on it, I get this page. Describe the features of the page. Here is the text box for the search engine. To work the search engine I type keywords, which are words that describe the subject I'm researching. I'd like some information on the painting style of the artist Picasso, so I use that name for my keyword. I type *Picasso* into the text box. Now I click Go. I get a long list of Web sites. This one is about the life of Picasso and this one is about his influence on other artists. Here is one about his style of painting, so I'll click on this site. I'll write some of the facts I found to remember them. To do more research, I click on the Back arrow at the upper left corner. That takes me back to the list of sites so I can choose another one.

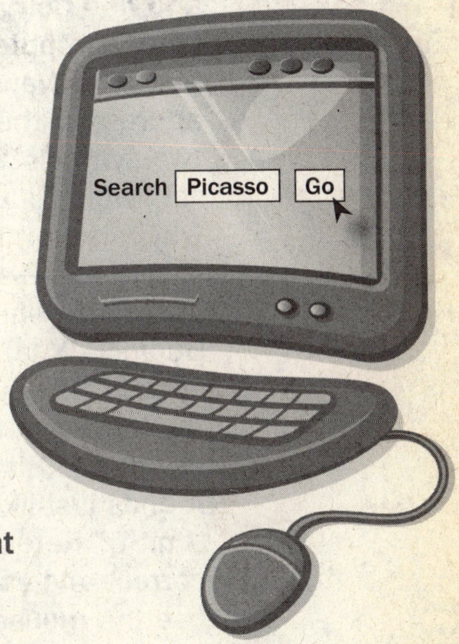

Guide practice Now it's your turn. Where do I click to get into the search engine? Right here. Have the group decide on a topic they'd like to research and lead them in finding information about the topic by using a search engine. Be sure their topic is narrow enough so that when they retrieve the list of Web sites, they can scroll to the one that best fits their needs.

On their own Let's all practice using a search engine. Pick a topic and decide on your keywords. Write three facts you find from your search. As students use the search engine and navigate Web sites, circulate among them, providing feedback.

MANAGEMENT TIP

Prior to using the search engine, have students write a list of topics and possible keywords, and then show you their list for approval.

Technology Practice Station

Management Lesson 3 Sending E-mail

Materials computer with projection, student computers, chart paper, markers

Introduce Today we are going to practice sending an e-mail message. E-mail is a fast and easy way to communicate. How many of you have an e-mail address? Have you ever sent or received an e-mail message? **Place your computer and arrange the class so all students can see the computer or projection.**

Model **Model sending an e-mail.** First, I find the e-mail icon on the desktop and click on it. Then I look at the toolbar and find Compose. **Click on Compose or the equivalent. (Your computer may use other terms, such as Create or New Message.)** Next, I type in the address of the person I am writing to. There are two symbols always found in e-mail addresses: "at," which is up here above the two, and "dot," which is simply a period. In the "To" box I type in the address, [student@school.edu]. See how I press the shift key for "at." Now I click on Subject. What is my message about? Homework. **Type in *Homework*.** Now I click here to write my message. It starts just like a letter: "Dear [Student]." **Hit Enter and type a simple message.** It ends just like a letter too: ["Your teacher, Ms. Smith]." Reread the message to be sure that it is correct and says what you want it to say. Now I'll use the mouse to hit Send.

Write *Sending an E-mail* at the top of a piece of chart paper. What are the steps you take when sending an e-mail? **As students respond, record their observations on the chart.**

Guide practice Now it's your turn. **Have the group tell you the steps needed to send an e-mail, and follow their steps as you type.** Here's the desktop. Where do you click? On the e-mail icon. You're going to send a message to me, [teacher@school.edu]. **Continue the practice until the e-mail is sent.**

On their own Let's all practice sending an e-mail. Use my address. Send a message asking a question about this week's reading selection. **Have individuals work at computers, composing and sending an e-mail. As students type, circulate among them, providing feedback.**

MANAGEMENT TIP

Students who have computers at home may have a different e-mail program than the classroom program. Point out differences and help them become familiar with the program you're using. Model and provide corrective feedback as necessary.

Multi Practice Station

At the Multi Practice Station, students work on a variety of activities in the areas of art, drama, music, math, and health. These activities provide opportunities for students to extend concepts learned during the week by combining literacy with the arts, math, and health.

Setting Up the Practice Station

Provide a table or arrange a group of desks where students can create art projects.

- Gather art materials such as paper, markers, crayons, rulers, and any other items that are specific to the week's activity.
- Store materials in a plastic bin for easier clean up and storage.
- Restock items as necessary.

Student Routine

- **Art** Create a simple portfolio for storage of artwork samples. Staple two pieces of poster board together and decorate. Add samples of your artwork each week.
- **Drama** *Improvisation* is performing without a script and without preparation. Perform a dialogue between two of the characters from this week's selection, or discuss the topic or theme for three minutes.
- **Music** Keep a music journal listing the types of music you've heard at the station. List the title and artist of each piece and explain why you liked or didn't like the piece, as well as any other thoughts.
- **Math** Read through the entire problem, and then write the pieces of information given. Use what you know to help solve the problem.
- **Health** After completing each Health Station activity, write a health tip in your journal.

TEACHER TiP

- For art or science stations, provide plastic trays or placemats on which students can work. These give students an individual workspace, help contain materials, and simplify clean up.

Assessing Station Activities

Practice Station activities provide excellent opportunities for informal, ongoing assessments that are useful in guiding instruction. Effective station activities provide opportunities for students to engage in meaningful tasks that advance learning in all areas, especially reading and writing. Emphasize to students that activities completed in the stations are important and will be assessed. Use information gathered from these assessments to guide instruction for individuals, groups, or the entire class.

Assessment Suggestions

Observe Student Work

- Determine what you expect in terms of student behaviors and attitudes and develop checklists based on those expectations.
- Focus on one or more students each day and keep informal notes about behavior, motivation, performance, or any other information you think is significant.
- Document students' learning and work habits and record social interactions.
- Hold periodic, structured conferences with students about their work.
- Plan support that addresses a student's particular strength or need.
- Record any information that will help make instructional decisions. You may want to use the Observation Record on p. 31.

Create and Post Rubrics

- Create a rubric to assess how well students follow centers' directions.
- Use a rubric to assess student creativity and motivation.
- Post a rubric in the Writing Practice Station so that students are aware of assessment criteria for writing projects.

Establish Portfolios

- Help students establish portfolios for stations' activities in progress.
- Use portfolio contents as a measure of progress and growth over time.

Involve Students in Self-Assessments

- Have students evaluate their own work and set goals for improvement.
- Have students evaluate each other's work in pairs and groups.

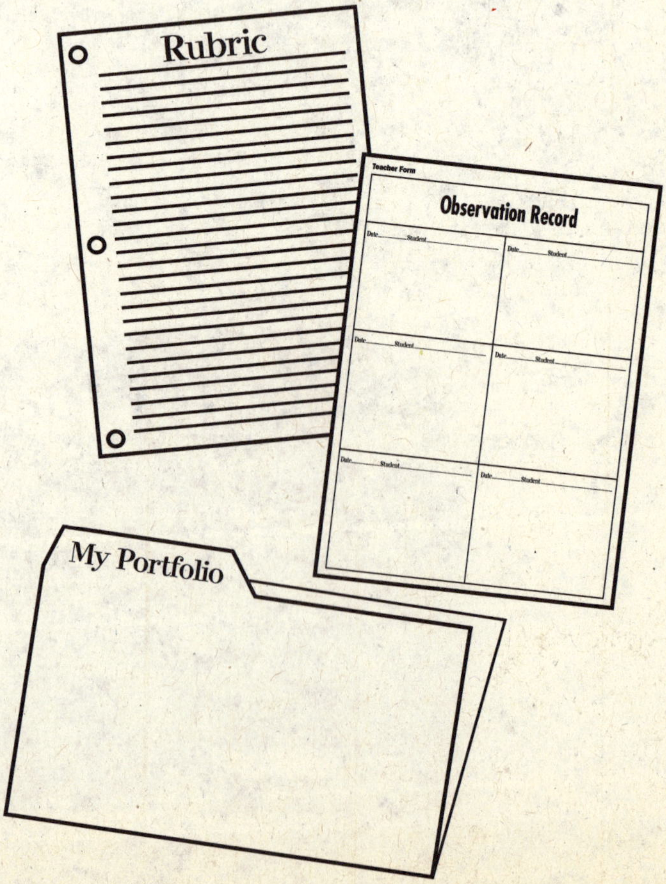

Teacher Form

Observation Record

Date........................ Student..	Date........................ Student..
Date........................ Student..	Date........................ Student..
Date........................ Student..	Date........................ Student..

Student Work Plans

What Are Student Work Plans?

Pages 33–62 contain lesson-specific reproducible work plans for students to use during their independent activity time. Each work plan lists the tasks that students will complete, in Practice Stations or independently, while you meet with small groups. The work plans help students remember their assignments, plan their time, and keep track of what they've done. Work plans allow students to take responsibility and will aid them in becoming successful independent learners.

How Do I Use the Student Work Plans?

Begin by explaining the activities in the Practice Stations to students. Then distribute copies of *My Work Plan* and review the tasks. Be sure students understand that they will check the box next to each task as they complete it. Remind students that if they finish an activity before time is up, they should answer the Wrap Up Your Week questions, read silently, or complete the Early Finishers activity. At the end of the week, you can collect students' work plans, or you can send them home.

If you prefer, you can customize a work plan for one or more students or for use during a particular lesson. For this purpose, a generic work plan can be found on p. 63.

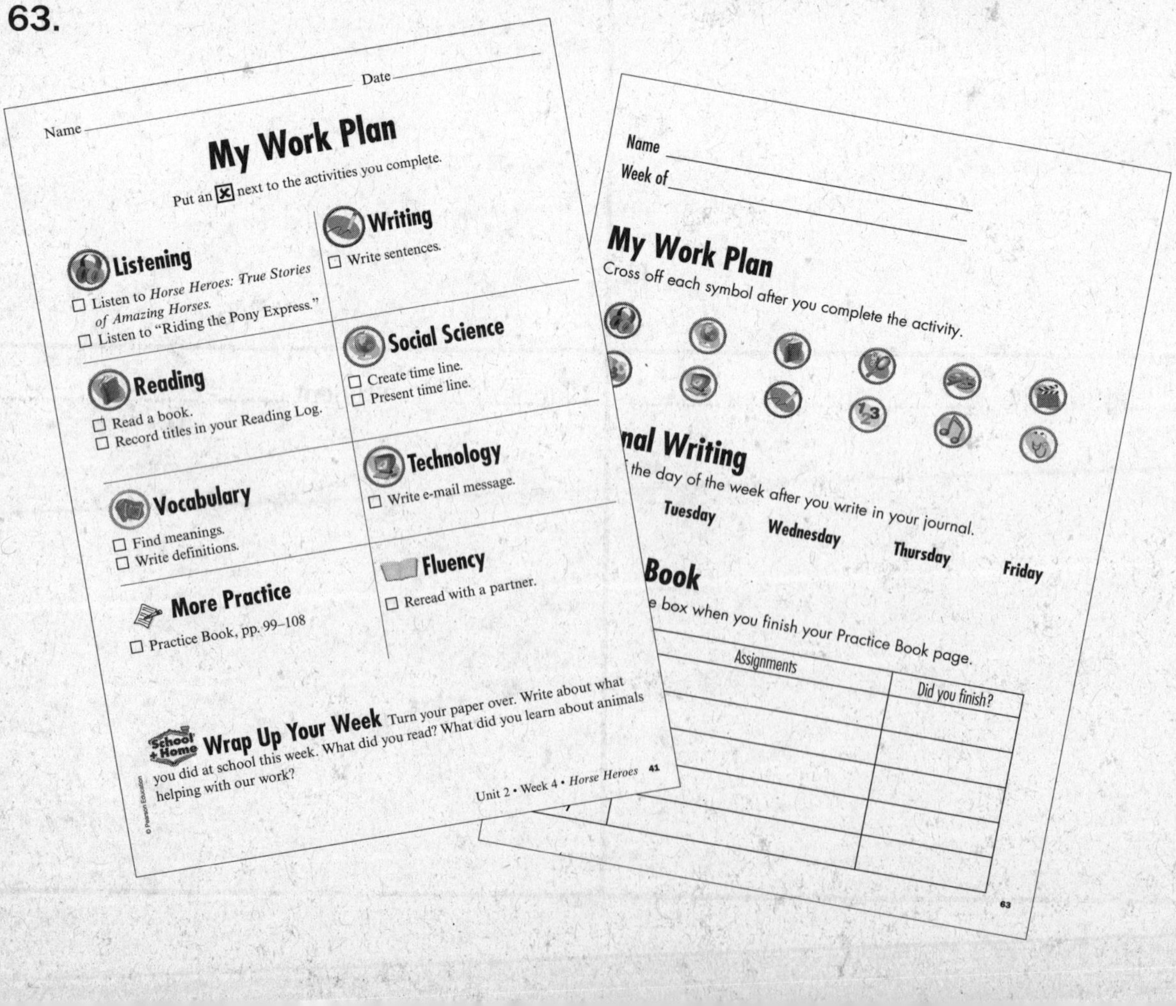

Name ____________________ Date ____________________

My Work Plan

Put an ☒ next to the activities you complete.

Listening

- ☐ Listen to *Yang the Youngest and His Terrible Ear.*
- ☐ Listen to "Gold Mountain."

Writing

- ☐ Write questions and answers.
- ☐ Label sentences.

Reading

- ☐ Read a book.
- ☐ Record titles in your Reading Log.

Social Science

- ☐ Find facts.
- ☐ Make fact sheets.

Vocabulary

- ☐ Find words.
- ☐ Discuss endings.

Technology

- ☐ Search the Internet.
- ☐ List facts.

More Practice

- ☐ Practice Book, pp. 1–10

Fluency

- ☐ Reread with a partner.

School + Home **Wrap Up Your Week** Turn your paper over. Write about what you did at school this week. What did you read? What did you learn about diversity?

Name ______________________ Date ______________

My Work Plan

Put an ☒ next to the activities you complete.

Listening

- ☐ Listen to *Hurry Freedom.*
- ☐ Listen to "The Lure of the West."

Writing

- ☐ Write sentences.
- ☐ Work with a partner.

Reading

- ☐ Read a book.
- ☐ Record titles in your Reading Log.

Social Science

- ☐ Write notes about success.
- ☐ Share with a partner.

Vocabulary

- ☐ Circle base words.
- ☐ Write paragraph.

Technology

- ☐ Find information about state park.
- ☐ Print map and directions.

More Practice

- ☐ Practice Book, pp. 11–20

Fluency

- ☐ Reread with a partner.

School + Home **Wrap Up Your Week** Turn your paper over. Write about what you did at school this week. What did you read? What did you learn about exploring new places?

Name ______________________ Date ______________

My Work Plan

Put an ☒ next to the activities you complete.

Listening

- ☐ Listen to *Grandfather's Journey.*
- ☐ Listen to "A Look at Two Lands."

Writing

- ☐ Write notes about a place.
- ☐ Write sentences.

Reading

- ☐ Read a book.
- ☐ Record titles in your Reading Log.

Social Science

- ☐ Locate items on map.
- ☐ Answer questions.

Vocabulary

- ☐ Write definitions.
- ☐ Discuss word use in text.

Technology

- ☐ Search for facts and sights.
- ☐ Complete T-chart.

More Practice

- ☐ Practice Book, pp. 21–30

Fluency

- ☐ Reread with a partner.

School + Home **Wrap Up Your Week** Turn your paper over. Write about what you did at school this week. What did you read? What did you learn about traveling in the United States?

Name ______________________ Date ______________

My Work Plan

Put an ☒ next to the activities you complete.

Listening

☐ Listen to *The Horned Toad Prince.*
☐ Listen to "The Fox and the Tiger."

Writing

☐ Complete T-chart.

Reading

☐ Read a book.
☐ Record titles in your Reading Log.

Science

☐ Make T-chart.
☐ Compare chart with partner's.

Vocabulary

☐ Find synonyms.

Technology

☐ Find picture.
☐ Paste picture into document and write caption.

More Practice

☐ Practice Book, pp. 31–40

Fluency

☐ Reread with a partner.

School + Home **Wrap Up Your Week** Turn your paper over. Write about what you did at school this week. What did you read? What did you learn about the Southwest?

Name ____________________ Date ____________________

My Work Plan

Put an ☒ next to the activities you complete.

Listening

- ☐ Listen to *Letters Home from Yosemite.*
- ☐ Listen to "Four Days in Yosemite."

Writing

- ☐ Revise paragraph.
- ☐ Work with a partner.

Reading

- ☐ Read a book.
- ☐ Record titles in your Reading Log.

Social Science

- ☐ Make chart.
- ☐ Complete chart.

Vocabulary

- ☐ Discuss differences.
- ☐ Write sentences.

Technology

- ☐ Find facts.
- ☐ Create fact sheet.

More Practice

- ☐ Practice Book, pp. 41–50

Fluency

- ☐ Reread with a partner.

School + Home **Wrap Up Your Week** Turn your paper over. Write about what you did at school this week. What did you read? What did you learn about the qualities of the West?

Name ______________________ Date ______________________

My Work Plan

Put an ☒ next to the activities you complete.

Listening

- ☐ Listen to *What Jo Did.*
- ☐ Listen to "Learning to Fly."

Writing

- ☐ Rewrite sentences.
- ☐ Work with a partner.

Reading

- ☐ Read a book.
- ☐ Record titles in your Reading Log.

Social Science

- ☐ Study government chart.
- ☐ Write notes.

Vocabulary

- ☐ Underline prefixes and suffixes.
- ☐ Write definitions.

Technology

- ☐ Find picture.
- ☐ Paste picture and write caption.

More Practice

- ☐ Practice Book, pp. 69–78

Fluency

- ☐ Reread with a partner.

School + Home **Wrap Up Your Week** Turn your paper over. Write about what you did at school this week. What did you read? What did you learn about appreciating the talents of others?

Name ____________________ Date ____________

My Work Plan

Put an ☒ next to the activities you complete.

Listening

- ☐ Listen to *Coyote School News.*
- ☐ Listen to "How to Start a School Newspaper."

Writing

- ☐ Take notes about the night.
- ☐ Take notes about the day.

Reading

- ☐ Read a book.
- ☐ Record titles in your Reading Log.

Social Science

- ☐ Create name.
- ☐ Brainstorm article names.
- ☐ Write list of interviewees.

Vocabulary

- ☐ Find meanings.
- ☐ Write sentences.

Technology

- ☐ Create masthead.
- ☐ Illustrate masthead.

More Practice

- ☐ Practice Book, pp. 79–88

Fluency

- ☐ Reread with a partner.

School + Home **Wrap Up Your Week** Turn your paper over. Write about what you did at school this week. What did you read? What did you learn about working together to achieve a goal?

Name ______________________________ Date ____________________

My Work Plan

Put an ☒ next to the activities you complete.

Listening

☐ Listen to *Scene Two.*
☐ Listen to "Front Porch."

Writing

☐ Write plurals.
☐ Work with a partner.

Reading

☐ Read a book.
☐ Record titles in your Reading Log.

Social Science

☐ Select hero and event.
☐ Describe characters.

Vocabulary

☐ Circle prefixes.
☐ Write definitions.
☐ Write paragraph.

Technology

☐ Create poster.
☐ Print poster.

More Practice

☐ Practice Book, pp. 89–98

Fluency

☐ Reread with a partner.

School + Home **Wrap Up Your Week** Turn your paper over. Write about what you did at school this week. What did you read? What did you learn about team accomplishments?

Name ______________________ Date ______________

My Work Plan

Put an ☒ next to the activities you complete.

Listening

- ☐ Listen to *Horse Heroes: True Stories of Amazing Horses.*
- ☐ Listen to "Riding the Pony Express."

Writing

- ☐ Write sentences.

Reading

- ☐ Read a book.
- ☐ Record titles in your Reading Log.

Social Science

- ☐ Create time line.
- ☐ Present time line.

Vocabulary

- ☐ Find meanings.
- ☐ Write definitions.

Technology

- ☐ Write e-mail message.

More Practice

- ☐ Practice Book, pp. 99–108

Fluency

- ☐ Reread with a partner.

School + Home **Wrap Up Your Week** Turn your paper over. Write about what you did at school this week. What did you read? What did you learn about animals helping with our work?

Name ______________________ Date ______________

My Work Plan

Put an ☒ next to the activities you complete.

Listening

☐ Listen to *So You Want to Be President?*

☐ Listen to "Our National Parks."

Writing

☐ Insert apostrophes.

☐ Work with a partner.

Reading

☐ Read a book.

☐ Record titles in your Reading Log.

Social Science

☐ Make list.

☐ Work with a partner.

Vocabulary

☐ Find meanings.

☐ Write definitions.

Technology

☐ Find facts.

☐ Work with a partner.

More Practice

☐ Practice Book, pp. 109–118

Fluency

☐ Reread with a partner.

School + Home **Wrap Up Your Week** Turn your paper over. Write about what you did at school this week. What did you read? What did you learn about the president's job?

Name ______________________ Date ______________

My Work Plan

Put an ☒ next to the activities you complete.

Listening

☐ Listen to *The Stranger.*
☐ Listen to "Time for a Change."

Writing

☐ Underline verbs.
☐ Label verbs.

Reading

☐ Read a book.
☐ Record titles in your Reading Log.

Science

☐ List characteristics.
☐ Write cause-effect chains.

Vocabulary

☐ Find meanings.
☐ Write definitions.
☐ Work with a partner.

Technology

☐ Find weather forecasts.
☐ Discuss weather forecasts.

More Practice

☐ Practice Book, pp. 137–146

Fluency

☐ Reread with a partner.

School + Home **Wrap Up Your Week** Turn your paper over. Write about what you did at school this week. What did you read? What did you learn about nature changing?

Name ______________________ Date ______________

My Work Plan

Put an ☒ next to the activities you complete.

Listening

- ☐ Listen to *Adelina's Whales.*
- ☐ Listen to "Sea Animals on the Move."

Writing

- ☐ Write purposes.
- ☐ Identify sentences.

Reading

- ☐ Read a book.
- ☐ Record titles in your Reading Log.

Science

- ☐ Draw whale.
- ☐ Label body parts.
- ☐ Write caption.

Vocabulary

- ☐ Find meanings.
- ☐ Write sentences.

Technology

- ☐ Find facts.
- ☐ Create fact sheet.

More Practice

- ☐ Practice Book, pp. 147–156

Fluency

- ☐ Reread with a partner.

School + Home **Wrap Up Your Week** Turn your paper over. Write about what you did at school this week. What did you read? What did you learn about animal migration?

Name ______________________________ Date ______________

My Work Plan

Put an ☒ next to the activities you complete.

Listening

- ☐ Listen to *How Night Came from the Sea.*
- ☐ Listen to "The Ant and the Bear."

Writing

- ☐ Write verbs.
- ☐ Work with a partner.

Reading

- ☐ Read a book.
- ☐ Record titles in your Reading Log.

Science

- ☐ Create T-chart.
- ☐ Complete T-chart.

Vocabulary

- ☐ Find meanings.
- ☐ Write sentences.

Technology

- ☐ Find facts.
- ☐ Create fact sheet.

More Practice

- ☐ Practice Book, pp. 157–166

Fluency

- ☐ Reread with a partner.

School + Home **Wrap Up Your Week** Turn your paper over. Write about what you did at school this week. What did you read? What did you learn about the pattern of day and night?

Name ______________________ Date ______________

My Work Plan

Put an ☒ next to the activities you complete.

Listening

☐ Listen to *Eye of the Storm.*
☐ Listen to "Severe Weather Safety."

Writing

☐ Create chart.
☐ Fill in causes and effects.

Reading

☐ Read a book.
☐ Record titles in your Reading Log.

Science

☐ Brainstorm ideas.
☐ Make poster.

Vocabulary

☐ Make chart.
☐ Complete chart.

Technology

☐ Find facts.
☐ Create table.
☐ Save document.

More Practice

☐ Practice Book, pp. 167–176

Fluency

☐ Reread with a partner.

School + Home **Wrap Up Your Week** Turn your paper over. Write about what you did at school this week. What did you read? What did you learn about storms?

Name ______________________ Date ______________

My Work Plan

Put an ☒ next to the activities you complete.

Listening

☐ Listen to *Paul Bunyan.*
☐ Listen to "A Very Grand Canyon."

Writing

☐ Write author's verbs.
☐ Discuss verb choice.

Reading

☐ Read a book.
☐ Record titles in your Reading Log.

Science

☐ Write explanations.
☐ Discuss explanations.

Vocabulary

☐ Underline suffixes.
☐ Write about suffixes.

Technology

☐ Create T-chart.
☐ Select most accurate Web site.

More Practice

☐ Practice Book, pp. 177–186

Fluency

☐ Reread with a partner.

School + Home **Wrap Up Your Week** Turn your paper over. Write about what you did at school this week. What did you read? What did you learn about changes in nature?

Name ____________________ Date ____________

My Work Plan

Put an ☒ next to the activities you complete.

Listening

- ☐ Listen to *The Houdini Box.*
- ☐ Listen to "So You Want to Be an Illusionist."

Writing

- ☐ Write adjectives.
- ☐ Work with a partner.

Reading

- ☐ Read a book.
- ☐ Record titles in your Reading Log.

Social Science

- ☐ Answer questions.
- ☐ Write page numbers.

Vocabulary

- ☐ Write synonyms and antonyms.
- ☐ Work with a partner.

Technology

- ☐ Find optical illusion.
- ☐ Create document with picture.

More Practice

- ☐ Practice Book, pp. 205–214

Fluency

- ☐ Reread with a partner.

School + Home **Wrap Up Your Week** Turn your paper over. Write about what you did at school this week. What did you read? What did you learn about perception?

Name ____________________ Date ____________

My Work Plan

Put an ☒ next to the activities you complete.

Listening

☐ Listen to *Encantado: Pink Dolphin of the Amazon.*

☐ Listen to "Mysterious Animals."

Writing

☐ Write main ideas.

☐ Work with a partner.

Reading

☐ Read a book.

☐ Record titles in your Reading Log.

Science

☐ Create T-chart.

☐ Complete T-chart.

Vocabulary

☐ Find meanings.

☐ Identify meaning in text.

Technology

☐ Search Internet and encyclopedia.

☐ Create T-chart.

More Practice

☐ Practice Book, pp. 215–224

Fluency

☐ Reread with a partner.

School + Home **Wrap Up Your Week** Turn your paper over. Write about what you did at school this week. What did you read? What did you learn about animal behavior?

Name ______________________ Date ______________

My Work Plan

Put an ☒ next to the activities you complete.

Listening

☐ Listen to *Navajo Code Talkers.*
☐ Listen to "Your Own Secret Language."

Writing

☐ Rewrite sentences.

Reading

☐ Read a book.
☐ Record titles in your Reading Log.

Social Science

☐ Create cipher.
☐ Decode cipher.

Vocabulary

☐ Create chart.
☐ Complete chart.

Technology

☐ Find answers.
☐ Create fact sheet.

More Practice

☐ Practice Book, pp. 225–234

Fluency

☐ Reread with a partner.

School + Home **Wrap Up Your Week** Turn your paper over. Write about what you did at school this week. What did you read? What did you learn about secret codes?

Name ______________________ Date ______________

My Work Plan

Put an ☒ next to the activities you complete.

Listening

☐ Listen to *Seeker of Knowledge.*
☐ Listen to "Making Mummies."

Writing

☐ Write instructions.

Reading

☐ Read a book.
☐ Record titles in your Reading Log.

Social Science

☐ Create chart.

Vocabulary

☐ Underline roots.
☐ Write meanings of roots.

Technology

☐ Find names.
☐ Find facts.

More Practice

☐ Practice Book, pp. 235–244

Fluency

☐ Reread with a partner.

School + Home **Wrap Up Your Week** Turn your paper over. Write about what you did at school this week. What did you read? What did you learn about communication?

Name ______________________ Date ______________

My Work Plan

Put an ☒ next to the activities you complete.

Listening

☐ Listen to *Encyclopedia Brown.*
☐ Listen to "Young Detectives of Potterville Middle School."

Writing

☐ Write contractions.
☐ Work with a partner.

Reading

☐ Read a book.
☐ Record titles in your Reading Log.

Science

☐ Make T-chart.
☐ Complete T-chart.

Vocabulary

☐ Write synonyms.
☐ Write antonyms.

Technology

☐ Write report.
☐ Format report.

More Practice

☐ Practice Book, pp. 246–254

Fluency

☐ Reread with a partner.

School + Home **Wrap Up Your Week** Turn your paper over. Write about what you did at school this week. What did you read? What did you learn about solving problems through attention to detail?

Name ______________________________ Date ______________

My Work Plan

Put an ☒ next to the activities you complete.

Listening

☐ Listen to *Smokejumpers: Life Fighting Fires.*

☐ Listen to "The Lookout."

Writing

☐ Explain meaning.

☐ Work with a partner.

Reading

☐ Read a book.

☐ Record titles in your Reading Log.

Science

☐ Make T-chart.

☐ Fill in causes and effects.

Vocabulary

☐ Find meanings.

☐ Write definitions.

Technology

☐ Find and write answers.

☐ Compare answers.

More Practice

☐ Practice Book, pp. 273–282

Fluency

☐ Reread with a partner.

School + Home **Wrap Up Your Week** Turn your paper over. Write about what you did at school this week. What did you read? What did you learn about emergencies?

Name ______________________ Date ______________

My Work Plan

Put an ☒ next to the activities you complete.

Listening

- ☐ Listen to *Lost City: The Discovery of Machu Picchu.*
- ☐ Listen to "Riding the Rails."

Writing

- ☐ Make chart.
- ☐ Complete chart.

Reading

- ☐ Read a book.
- ☐ Record titles in your Reading Log.

Social Science

- ☐ Find facts.
- ☐ Make travel brochure.

Vocabulary

- ☐ Write sentences.

Technology

- ☐ Find facts.
- ☐ Write e-mail message.
- ☐ Attach picture and send.

More Practice

- ☐ Practice Book, pp. 283–292

Fluency

- ☐ Reread with a partner.

School + Home **Wrap Up Your Week** Turn your paper over. Write about what you did at school this week. What did you read? What did you learn about exploring ancient civilizations?

Name ______________________ Date ______________

My Work Plan

Put an ☒ next to the activities you complete.

Listening

- ☐ Listen to *Cliff Hanger.*
- ☐ Listen to "Rock Climbing."

Writing

- ☐ Rewrite sentences.
- ☐ Work with a partner.

Reading

- ☐ Read a book.
- ☐ Record titles in your Reading Log.

Science

- ☐ Make diagram.
- ☐ Label diagram.

Vocabulary

- ☐ Write clues.
- ☐ Work with a partner.

Technology

- ☐ Find facts.
- ☐ Create fact sheet.

More Practice

- ☐ Practice Book, pp. 293–302

Fluency

- ☐ Reread with a partner.

School + Home **Wrap Up Your Week** Turn your paper over. Write about what you did at school this week. What did you read? What did you learn about being a hero?

Name ________________________________ Date ____________________

My Work Plan

Put an ☒ next to the activities you complete.

Listening

- ☐ Listen to *Antarctic Journal: Four Months at the Bottom of the World.*
- ☐ Listen to "Swimming Towards Ice."

Writing

- ☐ Create chart.
- ☐ Complete chart.

Reading

- ☐ Read a book.
- ☐ Record titles in your Reading Log.

Science

- ☐ Write statements.
- ☐ Work with a partner.

Vocabulary

- ☐ Write sentences.

Technology

- ☐ Write notes.
- ☐ Make poster.

More Practice

- ☐ Practice Book, pp. 303–312

Fluency

- ☐ Reread with a partner.

School + Home **Wrap Up Your Week** Turn your paper over. Write about what you did at school this week. What did you read? What did you learn about harsh climates?

Name ______________________ Date ______________

My Work Plan

Put an ☒ next to the activities you complete.

Listening

☐ Listen to *Moonwalk.*
☐ Listen to "A Walk on the Moon."

Writing

☐ Rewrite sentences.

Reading

☐ Read a book.
☐ Record titles in your Reading Log.

Science

☐ Find space terms.
☐ Make glossary.

Vocabulary

☐ Perform tasks.
☐ Work with a partner.

Technology

☐ Find details.
☐ Write e-mail message.

More Practice

☐ Practice Book, pp. 313–322

Fluency

☐ Reread with a partner.

School + Home **Wrap Up Your Week** Turn your paper over. Write about what you did at school this week. What did you read? What did you learn about the moon?

Name ____________________ Date ____________

My Work Plan

Put an ☒ next to the activities you complete.

Listening

- ☐ Listen to *My Brother Martin.*
- ☐ Listen to "Hopes and Dreams of Young People."

Writing

- ☐ Rewrite story.
- ☐ Work with a partner.

Reading

- ☐ Read a book.
- ☐ Record titles in your Reading Log.

Social Science

- ☐ Find laws.
- ☐ Make T-chart.
- ☐ Discuss Jim Crow laws.

Vocabulary

- ☐ Underline base words.
- ☐ Write new words.

Technology

- ☐ Find information.
- ☐ Make and illustrate fact sheet.

More Practice

- ☐ Practice Book, pp. 341–350

Fluency

- ☐ Reread with a partner.

School + Home **Wrap Up Your Week** Turn your paper over. Write about what you did at school this week. What did you read? What did you learn about equal opportunities?

Name ______________________ Date ______________

My Work Plan

Put an ☒ next to the activities you complete.

Listening

- ☐ Listen to *Jim Thorpe's Bright Path.*
- ☐ Listen to "Special Olympics, Spectacular Athletes."

Writing

- ☐ Rewrite sentences.
- ☐ Work with a partner.

Reading

- ☐ Read a book.
- ☐ Record titles in your Reading Log.

Social Science

- ☐ Find facts.
- ☐ Make list.
- ☐ Discuss discrimination.

Vocabulary

- ☐ Write meanings; circle one.
- ☐ Write sentences.
- ☐ Work with a partner.

Technology

- ☐ Find information.
- ☐ Create time line.

More Practice

- ☐ Practice Book, pp. 351–360

Fluency

- ☐ Reread with a partner.

School + Home **Wrap Up Your Week** Turn your paper over. Write about what you did at school this week. What did you read? What did you learn about challenges?

Name ____________________ Date ____________________

My Work Plan

Put an ☒ next to the activities you complete.

Listening

- ☐ Listen to *How Tía Lola Came to ~~Visit~~ Stay.*
- ☐ Listen to "The Difficult Art of Hitting."

Writing

- ☐ Write sentences.
- ☐ Work with a partner.

Reading

- ☐ Read a book.
- ☐ Record titles in your Reading Log.

Social Science

- ☐ Create T-chart.
- ☐ Complete T-chart.

Vocabulary

- ☐ Find meanings.
- ☐ Write report.

Technology

- ☐ Find Spanish words.
- ☐ Make glossary.

More Practice

- ☐ Practice Book, pp. 361–370

Fluency

- ☐ Reread with a partner.

School + Home **Wrap Up Your Week** Turn your paper over. Write about what you did at school this week. What did you read? What did you learn about coming to a new culture?

Name ______________________________ Date ____________________

My Work Plan

Put an ☒ next to the activities you complete.

Listening

☐ Listen to *Dream Water.*
☐ Listen to "The Hero's Quest."

Writing

☐ Rewrite scene as story.
☐ Work with a partner.

Reading

☐ Read a book.
☐ Record titles in your Reading Log.

Social Science

☐ Make and complete chart.
☐ Work with a partner.

Vocabulary

☐ Make T-chart.
☐ Complete T-chart.

Technology

☐ Write paragraph.
☐ Save document.

More Practice

☐ Practice Book, pp. 371–380

Fluency

☐ Reread with a partner.

School + Home **Wrap Up Your Week** Turn your paper over. Write about what you did at school this week. What did you read? What did you learn about achieving goals?

Name ______________________ Date ______________

My Work Plan

Put an ☒ next to the activities you complete.

Listening

- ☐ Listen to *The Man Who Went to the Far Side of the Moon.*
- ☐ Listen to "195 Days in Space."

Writing

- ☐ Rewrite sentences.

Reading

- ☐ Read a book.
- ☐ Record titles in your Reading Log.

Social Science

- ☐ Select objects.
- ☐ Work with another group.

Vocabulary

- ☐ Write definitions.
- ☐ Work with a partner.

Technology

- ☐ Find information.
- ☐ Create fact sheet.

More Practice

- ☐ Practice Book, pp. 381–390

Fluency

- ☐ Reread with a partner.

School + Home **Wrap Up Your Week** Turn your paper over. Write about what you did at school this week. What did you read? What did you learn about space exploration?

Name ________________________________

Week of ______________________________

My Work Plan

Cross off each symbol after you complete the activity.

Journal Writing

Cross off the day of the week after you write in your journal.

Monday **Tuesday** **Wednesday** **Thursday** **Friday**

Practice Book

Draw an X in the box when you finish your Practice Book page.

	Assignments	Did you finish?
Monday		
Tuesday		
Wednesday		
Thursday		
Friday		

Name ______________________

My Reading Log

Date	Title	Author	Genre	Minutes Read	Pages Read	My Opinion